Dedicate
and Celebrate!

Dedicate and Celebrate!
A Messianic Jewish Guide to Hanukkah

Barry Rubin and Family

Lederer Books
a division of
Messianic Jewish Publishers
Baltimore

Printed in the United States of America

08 07 06 05 04   7 6 5 4 3
ISBN 1-880226-83-9

Library of Congress Control Number: 2002278565

Published by
Lederer Books
a division of
Messianic Jewish Publishers
6204 Park Heights Ave.
Baltimore, Maryland 21215
(410) 358-6471

Distributed by
Messianic Jewish Resources International
Order line: (800) 410-7367
E-mail: lederer@messianicjewish.net
Website: www.messianicjewish.net

Introduction

Barry (Baruch) Rubin

The only place in the Bible that Hanukkah is mentioned by name is John 10:22. Messiah was in the Temple for the "feast of dedication," as many translations render the Greek word *eng-kai-nia*. This Greek word translates the Hebrew *hanukkah*. Both words convey the idea of "consecration" or "dedication." Because Messiah connected with Hanukkah, we believe that Christians, as well as Jews, can enjoy this celebration, all the more if its eternal importance is understood.

The focus of the holiday is the re-dedication of the Temple of the Lord about 160 years before Messiah's birth. God rescued his people, and preserved biblical Judaism. Without this, the prophetic fulfillment pertaining to the birth of Messiah could not have happened. Without Jews, Messiah could not have been born through the tribe of Judah, as a descendant of King David.

I've invited my family to participate with me in sharing this, one of our favorite holidays, with you. My wife, Steffi, a well-known graphic artist, has offered some wonderful illustrations to help convey Hanukkah to you; she has also written children's materials that appear later in this book. She's also a wonderful cook and has included several recipes unique to Hanukkah. Caution: don't eat too much of this; these are *not* fat-free recipes.

Our older daughter, Rebecca, an accomplished pianist, has pulled together some of the traditional Hanukkah songs that help tell the story. You'll enjoy singing them. Our younger daughter, Shira, an accomplished singer and "party-person," has written out the instructions for the *dreydel* game, a game developed to teach the story of God's miraculous redemption of the Jewish people.

I hope you will enjoy learning about this very special holiday, a day on which both Christians and Jews can celebrate.

Background

Solomon's Temple—the first Temple—was majestic and magnificent, but it was destroyed when the people of Israel were taken captive by the Babylonians in 586 B.C.E.

The books of Ezra, Haggai, Zechariah, and Nehemiah recount the building of the Second Temple, after the Jewish people returned from exile in Babylon. This Temple, built under Ezra's leadership, was dedicated approximately 450 years before Messiah. Within a few centuries, this Temple was profaned and desecrated by God's enemies. The dedication after the desecration gave rise to the holiday we now call Hanukkah, which means "dedication."

First and Second Maccabees (apocryphal books), Josephus in his *Antiquites*, and The Talmud (tractate Shabbat 21b), tell the story of this holiday. Also, Daniel 8 records the prophet's vision of the future, a vision that precisely foretells the events of Hanukkah.

What is the history of Hanukkah?

History records that Alexander the Great conquered most of the known world several centuries before Messiah's birth. After Alexander died, his kingdom was divided between his four generals. The Syrian-Greeks (the Seleucids) and the Egyptian-Greeks (the Ptolomies), two of the four kingdoms, often battled each other over Israel. Ultimately, the Syrian-Greeks won. When their ruler died, a man named Antiochus took over his kingdom, which contained what Daniel calls "the Beautiful Land"—Israel.

In order to subjugate the Jews, Antiochus, who called himself *Epiphanes*, meaning "God manifest," began to outlaw Jewish customs and observances such as Sabbath, circumcision, and kosher laws. He reasoned that if he could get the Jews to give up their "strange" ways, he could homogenize his country and better control it. He didn't want any religious practices except the Greek (Hellenistic) ways.

He continued to Hellenize the Hebrews. He destroyed Torah scrolls, placed heathen altars everywhere, made Jews bow down before Greek gods, placed a statue of Jupiter in the Temple, and finally sacrificed a pig in the Holy of Holies. That was the last straw.

First Maccabees states, "Now the fifteenth day of the month [Kislev—November/ December], in the hundred forty and fifth year, they [the Syrian-Greeks] set up the abomination of desolation upon the altar, and builded idol altars throughout the cities of Juda on every side" (1:54). This was the pagan Saturnalia ceremony, in which a pig was sacrificed in the Holy of Holies, the place of God's Presence.

In the small town of Modin, a man went to sacrifice to the heathen gods according to the law of the land. Mattathias, a righteous priest of Israel, a descendent of Moses' brother Aaron, an observant man of God, could not take it any longer. Just as Pinchas (Phineas) had done a millennium before him, when unholiness was being foisted upon Israel (Num. 25:6–9), Mattathias rose up and killed the Jew who was sacrificing to the gods of Greece.

He knew that this would begin the revolt, and shouted, "Let all who are zealous for the Law [and the Lord] follow me!" Mattathias and his sons, led by Judah, mustered enough forces to eventually overthrow the Syrian-Greeks. All the sons of Mattathias joined together, as well as many other zealous Jews willing to wage guerrilla warfare until the Syrian-Greeks were overthrown. Judah and his brothers were called "Maccabees." In Hebrew, Maccabee means "hammer," an apt description of their guerilla tactics. Thus began the Maccabean revolt.

After a three-year struggle, ending in 165 B.C.E., the Temple was recaptured, restored, and rededicated. Hanukkah commemorates and celebrates the re-dedication of the Holy Temple, so despicably desecrated by Antiochus and his Syrian-Greek legions.

You can imagine, then, that this day has been observed with great joy by Jewish people. Not only does it recall the rescue of the Jews, it remembers the day when God was victorious over heathen Hellenism.

The dedication sacrifice, after the Temple was recaptured, repaired, and rededicated, occurred on the same day as the desecration:

> Now upon the same day that the strangers profaned the temple, on the very same day it was cleansed again, even the five and twentieth day of the month which is Kislev. And they kept eight days with gladness, as in the Feast of Tabernacles (2 Maccabees 10:5–6).

Interestingly, 25 Kislev was also the day the "foundation of *Adonai*'s temple was laid" (Hag. 2:18).

Tradition teaches that when the Temple was restored, only one vial of oil had the seal of the High Priest on it, indicating that it could be used in the Temple menorah, the candelabra. But the one day's worth of sacred oil miraculously lasted for eight days, long enough for more oil to be prepared, so that the Temple could be ritually purified.

Yeshua the Messiah caused two loaves of bread and a few fish to feed thousands. Miracles occur. If God, then, was trying to communicate his pleasure regarding the restoration of his house, he very well might have caused this miracle to happen.

Hanukkah in the book of Daniel???

The prophet Daniel was the first to describe Hanukkah, although not by name. He foresaw the events leading up to the military victory celebrated at this time of the year. This is recorded in Daniel 8.

He had a vision of animals—rams and goats. He saw horns—big ones and little ones. He saw stars. He saw armies. He saw the future. God wanted him to know what was coming in the Land of Israel. God wanted his people to have the confidence to stand up for him. The prophecy was given for a purpose—to encourage the people.

First, Daniel saw a ram with two horns (vv. 3–4). One of these horns was longer than the other, arising later; this horn would conquer the known world. History shows that the nation referred to, Media-Persia, did indeed conquer the world. Media came first; later Persia dominated and ruled the known world from Egypt to India. This is the interpretation offered by the angel Gabriel (v. 20).

Then Daniel saw a picture of a male goat from the west with a prominent horn between its eyes (vv. 5–7). This goat would roam the whole earth, not touching the ground. It would destroy the horns of the ram mentioned in vv. 3 and 4, and the ram itself. Horns represented power in ancient days.

Alexander the Great's quick conquest of the world is pictured in vv. 5–7. He would rapidly destroy Media and Persia, and rule enormous amounts of territory. Verse 21 mentions Gabriel's interpretation—this goat was the king of Greece—Alexander!

Next in Daniel's vision (v. 8) came four horns that replaced the horn of Alexander, just at the height of his power. These four horns would spread out toward the four winds of heaven, but would not be as powerful as Alexander.

As said previously, when Alexander the Great died, his territory was distributed among his four leading generals—Ptolemy in Egypt, Cassander in Macedonia and Greece, Lysimachus in Asia Minor, and Seleucus in Israel. None of the successors had the power of Alexander. This is precisely the interpretation given by Gabriel in v. 22, albeit without using their names.

Daniel's vision concludes. A small horn, then, would arise from one of the four horns and grow exceedingly great (vv. 9–12). Daniel observes that the small horn grew toward the south, the east, and the Beautiful Land. It grew toward the army of heaven, causing some of the army and stars to fall. This "little horn" claimed equality with the commander of the army (God), and removed the sacrifice from the commander, throwing down the commander's sanctuary, stopping the regular sacrifice. The little horn even "flung truth on the ground" (v. 12).

Verse 23 describes how this "little horn" would act. Not only would he claim to be God, precisely what Antiochus did when he gave himself the title *Epiphanes*, but he would be "skilled in intrigue." In fact, he would be "amazingly destructive, and he will destroy the mighty and the holy ones" [here referring to the Israelites]. He will succeed through craftiness and deceit, become swelled with pride, and destroy many people just when they feel the most secure. He will even challenge the prince of princes [Messiah]; but without human intervention, he will be broken" (vv. 24–25). This is what Antiochus did as he took over the kingdom containing the Beautiful Land.

This is the story of Hanukkah, recorded in the Book of Daniel.

How is Hanukkah celebrated?

Now we'll tell you some ways our family celebrates this holiday. It's one of our favorites, as it is for most Jews. You'll see why.

The Hanukkiyah
(Hah-noo-**kee**-ah)

The central symbol of Hanukkah is the *hanukkiyah*, a nine-branched *version of the menorah*. The menorah was the seven-branch candelabra that shed light in the otherwise dark Tabernacle and later the Temple. The Hanukkah menorah, the *hanukkiyah*, is nine-branched, in order to remember the 8-day miracle. (An additional candle is used to light the other eight.)

Initially, people celebrated Hanukkah by bringing palm branches to Jerusalem, as they did on Sukkot, the Feast of Tabernacles. This was an ancient custom, the same used by the masses when Yeshua made his "triumphal entry" into Jerusalem. Some say that the reason for using palm branches was to recapture the Sukkot celebrations lost during the three-year battle with Antiochus. Whatever the initial purpose, the traditional practice gave way to the lighting of candles. Hanukkah, then, also became known as the Feast of Lights.

There's no biblically "correct" way to light the candles. However, certain customs have developed. As with much in Judaism, there are variations.

Rabbi Hillel, one of two leading rabbis around Yeshua's time on earth, would begin the first night of Hanukkah lighting just one candle and adding a candle each night until there were nine candles blazing. Rabbi Shammai, the other leading rabbi, began with the *hanukkiyah* filled and lit. He then removed a candle every night for the eight nights of Hanukkah.

Since Shammai was more strict concerning other things of Jewish law, my family, and most Jews today, follow the school of Hillel. You might find it interesting that Hillel's teachings were quite similar to Messiah's teaching.

The shammash

Earlier, I mentioned that the *hanukkiyah*, unlike a traditional, seven-branch menorah, has nine candles. The ninth candle is set apart from the rest of the candles, usually higher. It's used to light the other candles, which is why it's called *shammash*, a Hebrew word meaning "servant."

My family sees in this a picture of Yeshua the Messiah. He was "set apart" from the rest of humanity. He was holy, separate, above us all. Yet, he stooped down to give light to humankind, and as the servant, he continually desires to give us light if we will only hold out our wicks to be lit. Yeshua is the light of the world.

Hanukkah is a time to say to Messiah the servant, "Light my light." The Torah, the written word of God, is a light to our paths; Yeshua, the living Torah, is the same. But we need to "dedicate" ourselves to following his ways. That will make our celebration of Hanukkah all the more meaningful, whether Jewish or Christian.

We light the candles

Just after sundown, the evening before the first full day of Hanukkah, we face the menorah and light the candle on the far right first. I add candles each night, from right to left, and, lighting the *shammash* first, light the rest of the candles from left to right.

We are careful not to use the light from the *hanukkiyah* for utilitarian purposes. The light is only to remind us of God's victory over paganism.

The great Jewish scholar (also a follower of Yeshua) Dr. Alfred Edersheim wrote that the Talmud says the light should be placed at the entrance of the home or room or maybe near a window. The *hanukkiyah* then testifies to God's faithfulness.

Even though on all other holidays the women light the candles, on Hanukkah the man or head of the house is to light the candles. The following prayers are recited as the candles are lit:

בָּרוּךְ אַתָּה, יְיָ אֱלֹהֵינוּ, מֶלֶךְ הָעוֹלָם, אֲשֶׁר קִדְּשָׁנוּ בְּמִצְוֹתָיו
וְצִוָּנוּ לְהַדְלִיק נֵר שֶׁל חֲנֻכָּה.

Barukh atah ADONAI, Eloheynu melekh ha'olam, asher kidshanu b'mitzvotav v'tzivanu l'hadlik neyr shel Chanukkah.

Blessed are you, LORD our God, king of the universe, who sets us apart by his commandments and commanded us to light the lights of Hanukkah.

בָּרוּךְ אַתָּה, יְיָ אֱלֹהֵינוּ, מֶלֶךְ הָעוֹלָם, שֶׁעָשָׂה נִסִּים לַאֲבוֹתֵינוּ
בַּיָּמִים הָהֵם בַּזְמַן הַזֶּה.

Barukh atah ADONAI, Eloheynu melekh ha'olam, she'asah nisim l'avoteynu bayamim hahem bazman hazeh.

Blessed are you, LORD our God, king of the universe, who has performed miracles for our fathers in those days, at this time.

On the first night the following prayer is added:

בָּרוּךְ אַתָּה, יְיָ אֱלֹהֵינוּ, מֶלֶךְ הָעוֹלָם, שֶׁהֶחֱיָנוּ וְקִיְּמָנוּ וְהִגִּיעָנוּ
לַזְּמַן הַזֶּה.

Barukh atah ADONAI, Eloheynu melekh ha'olam, shehecheyanu, v'kiy'manu, v'higi'anu lazman hazeh.

Blessed are you, LORD our God, king of the universe, who has kept us alive and sustained us and enabled us to reach this season.

Once the candles are lit, it's time to eat, sing, and play—in a word, celebrate!

Conclusion

The meaning of the word is a lesson in commitment

When, as individuals, we began our relationship with God, we learned that we must focus on God. Yeshua said, "Go in through the narrow gate; for the gate that leads to destruction is wide and the road broad, and many travel it; but it is a narrow gate and a hard road that leads to life, and only a few find it" (Matt. 7:13–14). So from the start we knew we needed to narrow, focus, dedicate ourselves to God.

The Israelites had to struggle and sacrifice to be dedicated to God. They had to fight and stand for his Word. To follow the Lord means to fight the good fight, as Rav Sha'ul (Rabbi Saul, the Apostle Paul) said. To be dedicated to God means to destroy that which would take us away from him and embrace that which draws us close to him.

So then the meaning of the word Hanukkah reminds us that we must be dedicated to, focused on, and narrowed toward our father in heaven.

My little d'rash (commentary)

Hanukkah is closely connected with the Temple of God. Yeshua's followers are called the Temple of the spirit of God. Rav Sha'ul compared believers to the Temple of God in several places.

With regard to the preciousness of his people, he wrote,

> Don't you know that you people are God's temple and that God's Spirit lives in you? So if anyone destroys God's temple, God will destroy him. For God's temple is holy, and you yourselves are that temple (1 Cor. 3:16, 17).

With regard to sexual immorality, Sha'ul said,

> Don't you know that your body is a temple for the *Ruach HaKodesh* who lives inside you, whom you received from God? The fact is, you don't belong to yourselves; for you were bought at a price. So use your bodies to glorify God (1 Cor. 6:19).

With regard to being yoked together with unbelievers, Paul preached,

What agreement can there be between the temple of God and idols? For we are the temple of the living God (2 Cor. 6:16).

With regard to Gentiles becoming fellow-citizens with God's chosen people, the great emissary to the Gentiles wrote,

> You have built on the foundation of the emissaries and prophets, with the cornerstone being Yeshua the Messiah himself. In union with him the whole building is held together, and it is growing into a holy temple in union with the Lord. Yes, in union with him, you yourselves are being built together into a spiritual dwelling-place for God! (Eph. 2:21)

Paul's message in all these statements was that believers are as holy as the Temple. And since the Temple was to be cleansed and dedicated unto the Lord, so, too, God's people, Jewish and non-Jewish, need to be dedicated to cleansing our precious temples, both physically, emotionally, and spiritually.

As we observe Hanukkah, let us dedicate our temples to God . . . and celebrate God's protection from his and our enemies. And let us wish each other a VERY happy Hanukkah! Now it's my family's turn to share with you about Hanukkah.

A Word from the Wife
Steffi (Yaffa) Rubin

Growing up in a Jewish neighborhood in the Bronx, December did not mean Christmas—it meant Hanukkah. As days grew shorter and shorter, the welcome brightness of the Festival of Lights cheered us in the gloomy onset of winter. Presents were small (my experience never included the common current practice of giving one gift for each of the eight days), but the excitement of bringing out and polishing the Hanukkah menorah was great.

As an only child, I had the privilege of selecting which of the brightly colored Hanukkah candles would be set into place and lit each day. Sitting with the entire box spread out before me, I would mull over the myriad of choices, deciding whether to go with the random-selection motif, the duotone effect (perhaps yellow and green) or the all-blue or all-magenta look.

The Hanukkah music would spin round on the hi-fi and the smell of *latkes* (potato pancakes) frying in oil would quickly permeate our small apartment, whose windows were shut tight again the cold Northeast temperatures.

It was the time of the year I would turn over my penny bank in preparation for the high stakes of the annual *dreydel* competition. Once you mastered the art of spinning the four-sided *dreydel* and reading the Hebrew letters, this game of chance was finally one that didn't favor the older or more experienced. Maybe I would win a lot more pennies—or, even better, chocolate Hanukkah *gelt* (money)!

My husband mentioned oil, the central element in the traditional Hanukkah celebration. The miracle of the oil particularly captured my child's imagination long before I could fathom how Mattathias and Judah overcame the incredible odds that faced the Maccabees. Long before I took offense at the arrogance of Antiochus. Long before I appreciated the tragedy of the Temple desecration and the faith of my ancestors.

For me, the miracle of the oil was like magic—God's sleight of hand—the enchantment that accompanies all timeless children's tales. It was like having only one bright Hanukkah candles one night and finding a whole boxful in the morning!

And so, in keeping with the story, oil figures prominently in the traditional Hanukkah delicacies: *latkes* and *sufganiyot*.

Latkes (Potato Pancakes)

You know you've hit middle age when all your opening paragraphs begin with recollections! Nevertheless . . . in the days before food processors it was almost a Hanukkah commandment that knuckles had to be grated in the course of grating the peeled potatoes for your potato *latkes*. My husband's family seemed to have shared this experience and whenever we bring up the subject of *latkes*, the notion is once more corroborated. But since the introduction of the food processor, many have exchanged this tradition for the ease of grating their potatoes electronically. The choice is yours. I might suggest that in order to keep the chain unbroken, you might try a batch of *latkes* the old-fashioned way, using a hand grater (an appliance which is aptly named!) just to get the full flavor of the *latke* experience.

One word more on the subject of oil and Hanukkah: you can always diet after New Years, so heat up the frying pan and let her rip! However, if you are about to keel over from clogged arteries, there is a special dispensation for baking *latkes* instead of frying—but don't leave out the oil altogether; it's the whole idea!

Latkes

3 cups of raw, grated potatoes
1 small grated onion
2 eggs, lightly beaten
1 tsp salt (to taste)
1 heaping tbsp of flour or *matzah* meal
1/4 tsp baking soda
1/8 tsp pepper (to taste)

oil for frying
sour cream or apple sauce

Peel and grate (by hand or by food processor) the potatoes and onion, squeezing out as much of the liquid as you can. Add the remaining ingredients in the first group.

Heat the oil in a frying pan, about 1/4" in depth. When hot, drop the *latke* mixture into the oil to fry. Note: the size of *latkes* vary quite a bit—from ones that look like *gezunteh* (healthy-sized) burgers, to those that look like the silver-dollar size pancakes you get at a diner. This will ultimately be up to you. If the latkes are served as a kind of dessert or side-dish, the little ones may work best. But if you regard them as the main dish, the burger-size might make more sense.

Fry them until they are crispy on the outside and cooked on the inside. Then place them on paper towels to absorb the extra oil. As to the yield, this will depend on the size of the *latkes*—anywhere from 8 large to 24 small ones. They can be served immediately (this is best—nice and hot and crispy) or stored and served later (definitely less desirable but sometimes necessary).

On sour cream vs. apple sauce: This is one of those preference things. I'm partial to sour cream; my husband's family preferred apple sauce. My suggestion? Try them both, then decide!

What in the world are Sufganiyot?

Here is one custom that was not part of my childhood, but is important to include. Whereas potato *latkes* are the mainstay of Jews that came from Eastern Europe and are, therefore, big with American Jews, Israeli Jews don't do *latkes*. They do *sufganiyot*—jelly donuts. Ah! I can hear your brains whirring and yes, you have probably already realized that donuts are the Middle East fried-in-oil Hanukkah alternative.

I generally am not much of a donut fan, but a holiday is a holiday. You can pick them up at your local Dunkin' Donuts or make your own. Here's how:

Sufganiyot

    1/2 cup margarine

    1 cup flour

    1 tbsp sugar

    4 eggs

    2 qt vegetable oil for frying (no, this is not a typo: these babies go through oil quicker than an old car!)

    12 oz fruit preserves (flavor of your choice!)

    1/4 cup confectioners' sugar

Place margarine and 1 cup water in a small saucepan over medium-high heat and bring to a boil. Stir in flour and sugar. Cook, stirring vigorously, just until mixture forms a ball. Remove from heat. Beat in eggs, one at a time. Stir until smooth and well-blended.

Heat oil in a medium saucepan over high heat until it's ready for frying. While making the pastries, adjust the heat to maintain the temperature. Carefully drop batter by slightly rounded tablespoonfuls into hot oil. Fry until puffed and golden brown on all sides, about 2 minutes.

Remove them from the oil and drain on paper towels; then place them on wire racks to cool.

Fill a pastry bag, fitted with a filling tip, with preserves. Insert tip into each doughnut and squeeze about 1/2 tablespoon of filling into each. Dust with confectioners' sugar and serve. *Sufganiyot* do not store well, so they are best eaten the day they are made. The recipe yields 24 *sufganiyot*.

Hanukkah Music
Rebecca (Rivkah) Rubin

What would a Jewish holiday be without music? Dull, bland, ho-hum, boring! Hanukkah, like just about every other holiday, has many songs associated with it. Music gives character to our celebration; it adds to our joy! We have read the Hanukkah story; our minds understand what we are commemorating. But the music helps our hearts really get in the mood to rejoice.

Some of our favorite songs are on the following pages. "Ma'oz Tzur" is a rousing hymn of God's deliverance. It is a traditional part of the Hanukkah liturgy, recited by our people through the ages to remember his saving power. In addition to the traditional lyrics, we have added a verse to express our thanks for our eternal deliverance through Messiah Yeshua.

"The First Night of Hanukkah" works well by itself at candle-lighting time or along with the "Living Hanukkah Menorah" presentation. This skit, which you will find on page 19, is a fun way for children to participate in the Hanukkah celebration. They can learn about the Maccabees, and they will have their own part to contribute to the festivities! Really, with the room lights out, it is a beautiful sight.

"Hanukkah, O Hanukkah" is a fun song which describes the warmth and laughter in the home during the holiday, as well as the Hanukkah customs, such as playing with dreydels (see page 17), watching the light of the Hanukkah candles, and eating fresh, hot, delicious *latkes*. This song also has a "Messianic" verse.

All these songs help make the festival enjoyable for adults and accessible for children. Some of my earliest memories involve being part of the "Living Hanukkah Menorah," and participating in the music that is an essential part of the Hanukkah celebration. These songs help to preserve the memory of this beautiful time and to keep it with us throughout the year.

So enjoy the music which makes this holiday complete!

Maoz Tzur (Rock of Ages)

Marchlike

Traditional

Ma - oz tzur y' shu - a - ti. L' cha na - eh l' - sha bey ___ ach.

Tik - kun beyt t' - fil - la - ti v'- sham to - dah n'- za bey ___ ach.

L'eyt tash-bit mat - bey - ach. V' - tzar ham-na - bey_____ ach.

Az eg - mor b' - shir miz-mor, cha - nu- kat ha - miz - bey____ ach.

Az eg - mor b' - shir miz-mor, cha - nu- kat ha - miz - bey____ ach.

Rock of ages, let our song praise thy saving power.
Thou, amidst a raging foe, wast our shelt'ring tower.
Furious, they assailed us, but thine arm availed us.
And thy word broke their sword
  when our own strength failed us.
And thy word broke their sword
  when our own strength failed us.

Rock of ages, stumbling stone, whom the
  builders rejected.
You've become the cornerstone whom the Lord
  has selected.
Lift your voice and praise him! Worship God,
  who raised him!
Shine his light through the night, till the
  day we gaze at him. (Repeat last line)

The First Night of Hanukkah

Moderately

Steffi Rubin

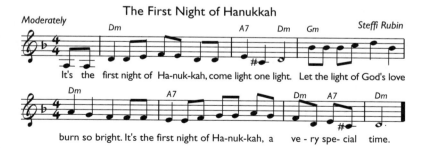

It's the first night of Ha-nuk-kah, come light one light. Let the light of God's love

burn so bright. It's the first night of Ha-nuk-kah, a ve - ry spe- cial time.

Other verses: It's the second night ... It's the third night ... etc.

Hanukkah, O Hanukkah!

Lively

Traditional

Ha - nuk-kah, O Ha- nuk-kah, come light the me-no-rah! Let's have a par-ty, we'll all dance the ho- ra. Ga-ther 'round the ta-ble, we'll give you a treat. Drey-del-ach to play with and lat - kes to eat. And while we are play- ing, the can-dles are bur-ning_ low. One for each night, they_ shed a sweet light, to re - mind us of days long a - go. One for each night, they_ shed a sweet light, to re - mind us of days long a - go.

Hanukkah, O Hanukkah, a time for reflection.
Gather 'round the burning lights and give your attention
To the one who is the light of the world.
Give it to Messiah, the light of the world.

And while we are praying to God, our Father and King,
His light will shine through our hearts to a world
That is longing for love he can bring.
His light will shine through our hearts to a world
That is longing for love he can bring.

The Game of Dreydel

Shira Rubin

Since Hanukkah is a celebration, it is important to have something special for the children to make it fun. Somewhere along the line the game of *dreydel* was invented for just this purpose. It is a fun game for all ages and it reminds us of the miracle of Hanukkah.

Begin by gathering together a group of your family and friends for this enjoyable Hanukkah game. Each person can bring his or her own favorite *dreydel,* or there can be just one that everyone uses to play the game.

Each person should start out with a good number of pieces of Hanukkah *gelt* (chocolate candy wrapped in gold foil, imitating the look of coins) or some other appropriate type of "coin"—pennies, raisins, nuts, bingo chips, or marbles. Every one begins by putting one piece into the "pot" in the middle of the circle of players.

Play begins with the youngest player in the circle; the others take turns going clockwise. (Being the youngest in our family, I always appreciated this rule.) Every person spins the *dreydel* when it is his or her turn. Spin the *dreydel* and watch to see which side faces up when the *dreydel* lands. The outcome of this spin will tell you what to do.

The *dreydel* is a four-sided top. Each side has a Hebrew letter. The four Hebrew letters on the *dreydel* are נ (*nun*), ג (*gimel*), ה (*hay*), and ש (*shin*). The letters stand for the four Hebrew words in the sentence *ness gadol hayah sham*, which translates, "a great miracle happened there," which is a reminder of what the holiday is all about.

When you spin the *dreydel* it will land on one of these letters. Here is what happens when it lands on each one:

- If the *dreydel* lands on the נ (*nun*)—nothing happens; play continues with the next person.

- If the *dreydel* lands on the **ג** (*gimel*)—the person spinning takes the entire pot. (After this happens, every player puts another piece into the pot to replenish it.)
- If the *dreydel* lands on the **ה** (*hay*)—the person takes half of the pot. (If the pot is uneven, you take the smaller half.)
- If the *dreydel* lands on the **ש** (*shin*)—you must put one of your pieces in the pot.

Many people use helpful little phrases to remember these rules, such as:

"*Nun, nun*, nothing's won."
"*Gimel, gimel*, get it all."
"*Hay, hay*, take half away."
"*Shin, shin*, put one in."

A great miracle happened...where?

Dreydels from Israel have one different letter on them than dreydels from other nations. There is no *shin* on the Israeli *dreydel*—can you think of why? Remember the phrase that the four letters stood for, "a great miracle happened there"? The *shin* stood for the word "there." Of course, if you are in Israel the great miracle didn't happen "there" but "here." So, instead of a *shin* there is a *peh*, which stands for the Hebrew word "*po*," meaning "here." Israeli dreydels declare "a great miracle happened *here*," because it happened in Israel. The letter *peh* has the same instructions in the *dreydel* game as does the letter *shin*. It is easy to remember to "pay" when your *dreydel* lands on *peh*.

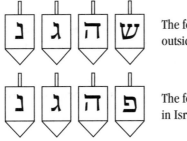

The four sides of *dreydel* outside of Israel

The four sides of *dreydel* in Israel

More fun and Games
Something for the Congregations
Steffi (Yaffa) Rubin

Congregations are the perfect places for production and pageantry. People enjoy participating in plays—especially children. It is so important to make holiday memories that will encourage our children to remember these important festivals and celebrations. This program can involve even the youngest of children and can be adapted according to your needs. The accompanying song can be found on page 15.

We have also included a poem that children can learn about Hanukkah. We used it with our Kindergarten–First Grade class. Each child learned a verse and recited it.

We made up a Hanukkah "Madlibs," also included (rules are on page 25).

Finally, there are some Hanukkah card designs for the little ones to color.

So enjoy! Holidays are *supposed* to be fun!

The Living Hanukkah Menorah
A Children's Program for Congregations

(Line up nine children across the front of the platform; put the tallest child in the middle—he or she is the shammash; *the rest of the children will be numbered 1, 2, etc., looking from the audience, starting from the left. Each child holds a flashlight with some red crepe paper twisted up in the shape of a flame taped over the light. As they begin, the middle child turns on his flashlight.)*

Middle child (shammash):

I am the shammash, the servant candle. I stand tallest of all the candles. Like the Messiah, who was the greatest of all, I bow down to share my light with others. Yeshua said he who would be greatest in God's kingdom must humble himself and be the servant of all.

All sing: It's the first night of Hanukkah, come light one light.
Let the light of God's love burn so bright;
It's the first night of Hanukkah, a very special time.

(During the song the shammash child walks over to child 1 and "lights" that child's light. That is, child 1 turns on his own flashlight. It stays on.)

Child 1:

I am the first candle. One stands for the one little jar of holy oil that the Maccabees found when they recaptured the Temple in Jerusalem. One small jar—with enough oil to burn in the Temple menorah for just one day. And yet, through a miracle of God, the oil burned on and on for eight days.

All sing: It's the second night of Hanukkah, come light 2 lights.
Let the light of God's love burn so bright;
It's the second night of Hanukkah, a very special time.

(During the song the shammash child walks over to child 2 and "lights" that child's light. It stays on.)

Child 2:

I am the second candle. Two stands for the two leaders of the Jewish revolt against the cruel ruler Antiochus. Mattathias and his son Judah refused to allow the evil king to destroy the Jewish people by destroying Jewish practices and worship. They stood against him and with God's help overcame the enemies of the Jewish people.

All sing: It's the third night of Hanukkah, come light 3 lights.
Let the light of God's love burn so bright;
It's the third night of Hanukkah, a very special time.

(During the song the shammash child walks over to child 3 and "lights" that child's light. It stays on.)

<u>Child 3:</u>

I am the third candle. Three stands for the three years of struggle that it took to overcome Antiochus and his evil rule. The Maccabees fought for three long, hard years until the Temple was recaptured and the Jewish people were allowed to worship once again, according to the ways of God.

All sing: It's the fourth night of Hanukkah, come light 4 lights.
Let the light of God's love burn so bright;
It's the fourth night of Hanukkah, a very special time.

(During the song the shammash child walks over to child 4 and "lights" that child's light. It stays on.)

<u>Child 4:</u>

I am the fourth candle. Four stands for the number of letters on the dreydel. The letters, Nun, Gimmel, Hay and Shin stand for "Ness Gadol Hayah Sham," a great miracle happened there. These letters remind us of the miracle of the oil that God performed during the days of the Maccabees.

All sing: It's the fifth night of Hanukkah, come light 5 lights.
Let the light of God's love burn so bright;
It's the fifth night of Hanukkah, a very special time.

(During the song the shammash child walks over to child 5 and "lights" that child's light. It stays on.)

<u>Child 5:</u>

I am the fifth candle. Five is the number of Mattathias' sons, the Maccabees. They were called Maccabees, which means "hammers." Because they were so outnumbered by the king's army, the Maccabees would hide in the hills and pounce down on the enemies like hammers. These surprise attacks proved to be a very good strategy.

All sing: It's the sixth night of Hanukkah, come light 6 lights.
Let the light of God's love burn so bright;
It's the sixth night of Hanukkah, a very special time.

(During the song the shammash child walks over to child 6 and "lights" that child's light. It stays on.)

Child 6:

I am the sixth candle. Six stands for the six "hallel" psalms that are read during Hanukkah. They are Psalm 113 through Psalm 118. "Praise *ADONAI*, you nations! Worship him, all you peoples! For his grace toward us is great, and *ADONAI*'s truth continues forever."

All sing: It's the seventh night of Hanukkah, come light 7 lights.
Let the light of God's love burn so bright;
It's the seventh night of Hanukkah, a very special time.

(During the song the shammash child walks over to child 7 and "lights" that child's light. It stays on.)

Child 7:

I am the seventh candle. There were seven branches of the menorah in the Temple. In the Bible seven is an important number. It stands for God. It stands for God's holy day, the Sabbath. Some believe that the seven branches of the menorah also represent the seven days of creation.

All sing: It's the last night of Hanukkah, come light 8 lights.
Let the light of God's love burn so bright;
It's the last night of Hanukkah, a very special time.

(During the song the shammash child walks over to child 8 and "lights" that child's light. It stays on.)

Child 8:

I am the eighth and last candle. Eight stands for the eight days of Hanukkah. Eight miraculous days when the little jar of oil, the one with just enough to last for one day, burned and burned for eight full days, long enough for the priests to prepare new holy oil. We celebrate Hanukkah for eight days and nights, and we rejoice over God's continuing faithfulness to his people.

Note: If you want to use small children for the menorah, you can have the children merely say "I am the first candle" etc., and use an older child or adult for the narration.

Nun Gimmel Hay and Shin

Nun, gimmel, hay and shin
Tell me now, what does that mean?
A great miracle happened there,
Many years ago.

Take your *dreydel*, make it spin
Tell the story, let's begin
We can tell the story
As we watch the candles glow.

Nun stands for NESS, which means
A MIRACLE, a special thing
That God did for the Maccabees
To make their oil last long

And gimmel is for GREAT, GADOL
The miracle that burned the oil
That lasted for eight nights
Though there was just enough for one.

Hay is HAYAH, it's for real
It isn't just a made-up shpiel
It HAPPENED through God's faithful power
To bless his Temple light.

And Shin is SHAM, that special place
Called Israel, God's land of grace
The great miracle that happened there
We celebrate tonight.

So each time that a *dreydel* whirls
To please a little boy or girl
We understand the message that
It teaches as we play.

Hanukkah Madlibs

Hanukkah is the Festival of _____ *(plural noun)* or the Feast of Dedication. The Hebrew word Hanukkah means _____ *(noun)*. The holiday begins on the eve of the _____th *(number)* day of the Hebrew month of _____ *(foreign word)* which corresponds approximately to the standard calendar month of _____ *(month)*. Hanukkah lasts for _____*(number)* days. During Hanukkah, _____ *(plural noun)* are exchanged among family and friends. Each evening as the _____ *(noun)* goes down one candle is lighted in a special nine-branched candle-holder called a _____ *(noun)* or _____ *(noun)*. Beginning on the second night one candle is added every night until the total reaches _____ *(number)* on the last night. The candles are lighted by a separate candle called the _____ *(noun)* or servant candle. The two books of Maccabees were written between the times of the _____ and _____ *(opposites)* Testaments. These books tell the story of Hanukkah. The word Maccabee means "_____" *(noun)* and it was the nickname given to the Jewish army. In the year 165 B.C.E., after a struggle of _____ *(number)* _____*(period of time)* led by two Jews named _____*(person's name)* and his son _____ *(person's name),* the Maccabees in Judea defeated Syrian tyrant _____ *(person's name)* the _____th *(number)*. This _____ *(adjective)* king had defiled God's Temple by setting up idols and by sacrificing a _____*(animal)* on the altar, which was not very kosher. When the _____*(plural noun)* had defeated the _____*(adjective)* king, they held festivities in _____ *(city),* and dedicated the _____ *(noun)* to God. According to tradition, the Maccabees entered the Temple to _____ *(verb)* it, but found only one small cruse of oil with which to light the Temple _____ *(noun).* _____ *(adverb),* the cruse provided them with oil for _____ *(number)* days. That is why we light the _____ *(noun),* play _____ *(plural noun),* sing _____ *(plural noun),* and give _____ *(plural noun)* — to celebrate the miracle of Hanukkah.

Hanukkah Madlibs

(These are the "correct" answers to the madilbs to the left.)

Hanukkah is the Festival of <u>Lights</u> or the Feast of Dedication. The Hebrew word Hanukkah means <u>dedication</u>. The holiday begins of the eve of the <u>25th</u> day of the Hebrew month of <u>Kislev</u>, which corresponds approximately to the standard calendar month of <u>December</u>. Hanukkah lasts for <u>eight</u> days.

During Hanukkah, <u>gifts</u> are exchanged among family and friends. Each evening as the <u>sun</u> goes down one candle is lighted in a special nine-branched candleholder called a <u>Menorah</u> or <u>Hanukkiah</u>. Beginning on the second night one candle is added every night until the total reaches <u>eight</u> on the last night. The candles are lighted by a special, separate candle called the <u>shammash</u>, or servant candle.

The two books of Maccabees were written between the times of the <u>Old and New</u> Testaments. These books tell the story of Hanukkah. The word Maccabee means <u>"hammer"</u> and it was the nickname given to the Jewish army. In the year 165 B.C.E., after a struggle of <u>three years</u> led by two Jews named <u>Mattathias</u> and his son <u>Judah</u>, the Maccabees in Judea defeated Syrian tyrant <u>Antiochus IV</u>. This <u>wicked</u> king had defiled God's Temple by setting up idols and by sacrificing a <u>pig</u> on the altar, which was not very kosher. When the <u>Maccabees</u> had defeated the <u>wicked</u> king, they held <u>festivities</u> in <u>Jerusalem</u>, and dedicated the <u>Temple</u> to God. According to tradition, the Maccabees entered the Temple to <u>clean</u> it but found only <u>one</u> small cruse of oil with which to light the Temple <u>lamp</u>. <u>Miraculously</u>, the cruse provided them with oil for <u>eight</u> days.

That is why we light the <u>menorah</u> , play <u>games</u>, sing <u>songs</u> and give <u>gifts</u> — to celebrate the miracle of Hanukkah.

RULES FOR PLAYING MADLIBS:

Madlibs is a fun and silly way to enjoy the holiday. Using the page on the left, ask a group of people for the appropriate part of speech; for example, "Give me a plural noun." They will say something like "slippers!" and you write that in the blank. When all the blanks are filled in, read the story aloud. We guarantee it will be riotous! Then, when all are calm, read the story above and remember the real tale of Hanukkah.

Happy Hanukkah

חֲנֻכָּה

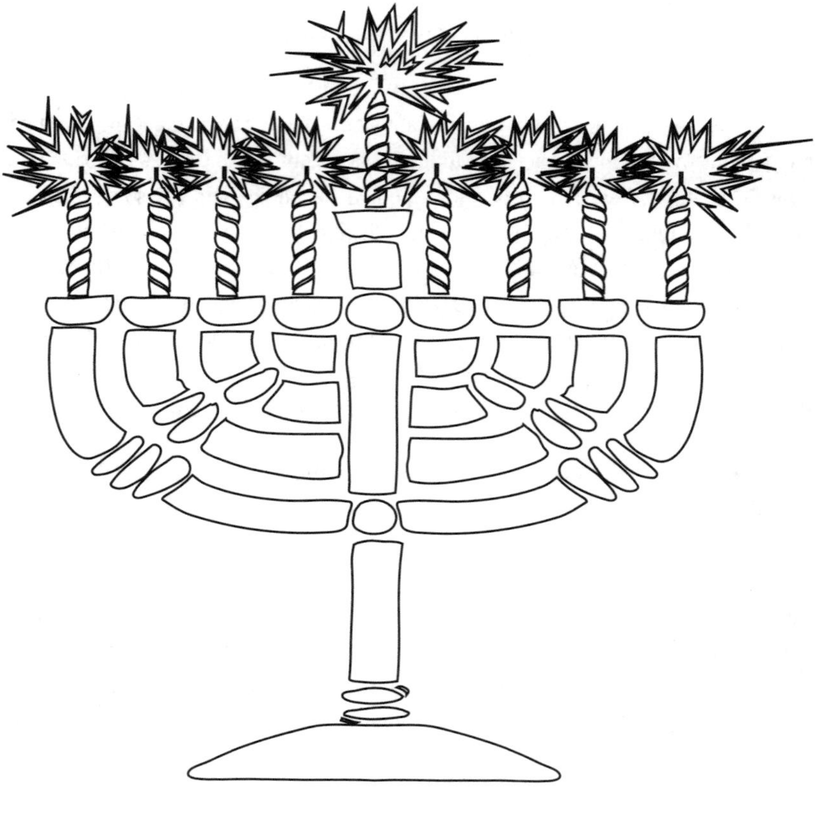

HAPPY
HAPPY
HAPPY
HAPPY

HANUKKAH!

Bibliography

Buksbazen, Victor. *The Gospel in the Feasts of Israel*. West Collingswood, NJ: The Friends of Israel, 1954.

Donin, Rabbi Hayim Halevy. *To Be a Jew: A Guide to Jewish Observance in Contemporary Life*. New York: Basic Books, Inc., Publishers, 1972.

Donin, Rabbi Hayim Halevy. *To Pray as a Jew: A Guide to the Prayer Book and the Synagogue Service*. New York: Basic Books, Inc., Publishers, 1980.

Fischer, John. *Messianic Servies for the Festivals and Holy Days*. Palm Harbor, FL: Menorah Ministries, 1992.

Gaster, Theodor H. *Festivals of the Jewish Year: A Modern Interpretation and Guide*. New York: Morrow Quill Paperbacks, 1952.

Goodman, Philip. *The Hanukkah Anthology*. Philadelphia: The Jewish Publication Society, 1992.

Kasdan, Barney. *God's Appointed Times: A Practical Guide for Understanding and Celebrating the Biblical Holidays*. Baltimore: Messianic Jewish Publishers, 1993.

Siegel, Richard, Michael Strassfeld, and Sharon Strassfeld. *The First Jewish Catalog: A Do-It-Yourself Kit*. Philadelphia: The Jewish Publication Society of America, 1973.

Zimmerman, Martha. *Celebrate the Feasts of the Old Testament in Your Own Home or Church*. Minneapolis: Bethany House Publishers, 1981.

Note

All Hanukkah products mentioned in this book, such as *hanukkiyahs*, candles, and *dreydels*, are available through Messianic Jewish Resources International. Call 800 410-7367 or visit www.messianicjewish.net.